All You Need to Know About Foreclosure

By Ade Asefeso MCIPS MBA

Second Edition

ISBN-13: 978-1499599909

ISBN-10: 1499599900

Publisher: AA Global Sourcing Ltd
Website: http://www.aaglobalsourcing.com

Table of Contents

Disclaimer

This publication is designed to provide competent and reliable information regarding the subject matter covered. However, it is sold with the understanding that the author and publisher are not engaged in rendering professional advice. The authors and publishers specifically disclaim any liability that is incurred from the use or application of contents of this book.

If you purchased this book without a cover you should be aware that this book may have been stolen property and reported as "unsold and destroyed" to the publisher. In this case neither the author nor the publisher has received any payment for this "stripped book."

Dedication

This book is dedicated to the hundreds of thousands of incredible souls in the world who have weathered through the up and down of recent recession.

To my family and friends who seems to have been sent here to teach me something about who I am supposed to be. They have nurtured me, challenged me, and even opposed me…. But at every juncture has taught me!

This book is dedicated to my lovely boys, Thomas, Michael and Karl. Teaching them to manage their finance will give them the lives they deserve. They have taught me more about life, presence, and energy management than anything I have done in my life.

Chapter 1: What is Foreclosure Know What it is and How to Avoid It.

Everyone is in need of money. Whether to refinance a business or to push through with a home improvement plan, they place their property or business on the line and go for a mortgage loan. But most simply use this method without knowing the risk involved which is foreclosure.

Prior to foreclosure- the act of mortgage

One good definition of a mortgage is the act of using a property or a business as a security for a monetary loan. In a legal sense, a mortgage loan is used to pay off an existing debt using a property of the same value to be used as a security. The term "lender" is often referred to as an entity that provides the amount for the mortgage loan, usually a bank or a lending company. The borrower will then be subjected to the terms and conditions stated by the lender such as interest rates, terms, and deadline of payment.

What is foreclosure?

Foreclosure happens when the bank or the lender sells or repossesses a property used in the mortgage loan, or a deed of trust, in which the owner fails to comply with his or agreement with the bank or lender. It is always important for the borrower to know the terms and conditions of the mortgage loan. Knowing information like interest rates, deadlines of payment, and other agreements and conditions between the lender and the borrower helps to avoid the risk of foreclosing the property to the lender.

Type of foreclosure

One type of foreclosure is the foreclosure by judicial sale. The sale of the property or business used in a mortgage will be supervised by the court and all the proceedings will be properly distributed by it. Since this type of foreclosure will be under legal jurisdiction, then all parties will be the first notified.

Usually, in case of a sale, the proceedings will be distributed accordingly by the court; first to satisfy the terms and conditions of the loans, other liens or parties involved, then finally to the mortgagor.

The most popular type of foreclosure is the foreclosure by power of sale. This involves the sale of the property by the mortgage holder and not under the legal jurisdiction of a court. Once the property or the business has been sold by the bank or the lender, then the proceedings will be distributed accordingly; first to the terms of the loan and then to the mortgagor.

The ancient form of foreclosure is called strict foreclosure. The mortgagor is informed by the court to pay the mortgage loan in a specific period of time. When the borrower fails to pay the debt by the said deadline, then the mortgage holder will then gain ownership and title of the property without any obligation to sell. This kind of foreclosure is the least practiced since it doesn't give any elbow room to mortgagor in getting his property, or any proceedings, back.

Avoid foreclosure - tips in getting a mortgage loan safely. In order to avoid foreclosure, the borrower must first determine the amount to be borrowed in which he or she deems payable. It's always best to borrow enough money for your needs or you might find it difficult to pay both the principal amount and the interest in the near future.

It is always prudent to check out various companies or banks that offer low interest rates on mortgage loans. Most companies and lending institutions can now be seen on the Internet so looking them up and comparing the best deals is now quite easy.

Another important method to take into consideration to avoid foreclosure is to use the services of a mortgage broker or a financial adviser. These people specialize in various mortgage loans and know everything about foreclosure. They can give you advice on the best deals for a loan and keep tabs on various terms and conditions to avoid a possible foreclosure on your property.

To avoid the possibility of foreclosing your property, it is always best to know all about the ins and outs of mortgage and foreclosure before you get into it.

If you are facing the tight economy head-on like a bulldog and continue to do well financially, you can consider yourself blessed that you are not facing home foreclosure.

If you are struggling with the shaky real estate market conditions, have become unemployed, or are facing some other financial setback, you may be facing a potentially scary and stressful home foreclosure.

If you do find yourself struggling to make your mortgage payments every month, the first thing you should realize is that you are not alone in your struggle. There are thousands of Americans facing the same or similar circumstances as the housing boom has transformed into the home foreclosure boom.

The second thing you should realize is that there are options available to you. It may seem like the most horrendous thing in the world to be looking at a home foreclosure possibility, and indeed, it is definitely serious. At the same time, a home foreclosure does not have to mean the end of life as you have always known it.

The third thing you should realize is that the bank does not want your house. Banks and other financial institutions are not in the real estate market. They are in the banking and finance industry, and foreclosures are expensive and time-consuming to them. This being the case, many lenders are willing to help you avoid a home foreclosure if at all possible. If you are embarrassed to admit your financial woes, get over it and start helping yourself as soon as possible. Keeping your home is the best thing for you and your bank.

If you have missed only one mortgage payment, you will probably receive a notice from your bank. Do not ignore it. Burying your head in the sand will not work. If you totally ignore your financial institution's correspondence, they are likely to believe that there is no way they will ever get payment from you and will be less likely to work with you to avoid home foreclosure if you wait too long.

If you are behind on your mortgage payments or expect that you will be due to some personal circumstance, it is time to dig out your loan agreement. Many mortgages haves clauses that actually provide alternatives to foreclosure if certain procedures are followed. Very few people know all the details of their loans so get out your paperwork and know what is going on with your loan.

There are professional organizations and attorneys to help you, as well. If you think that you can't afford to hire professional help, it still pays to look into the idea. Professionals who specialize in avoiding home foreclosure know that financial difficulties are what bring clients to them. They probably have a way to help you manage both the foreclosure stop and their fees.

Probably one of the easiest and most common ways to avoid home foreclosure is to modify the terms of your loan. A real estate attorney or home foreclosure expert can likely help you to re-negotiate your mortgage with terms you are able to meet and save both you and the bank all the trouble of a home foreclosure. Most financial institutions are more than willing to come to a mutual, agreeable meeting of the minds in order to stay out of the house-selling market and do what they do best – banking.

Chapter 2: Foreclosure; an Overview

Most lending institutions today prefer the process of a Non-Judicial Foreclosure since it doesn't have any complications or legal proceedings attached to it. Simply put, this kind of foreclosure is between both the lender and the borrower.

What is a non-judicial foreclosure?

Non-Judicial Foreclosure is a type of foreclosure without any court intervention. As defined above, this kind of foreclosure is simply between the lender and the borrower, or other persons with connections to the transaction like a mortgage broker or a financial adviser.

When the mortgage has reached its maturity date and the borrower has yet to fulfill the payment of the debt, then the lender will send a Notice of Default informing the borrower that the deadline for the said mortgage has elapsed.

In the event of a mortgage that requires payments on a specific date, failure to make those payments as specified can result in a default foreclosure.

If the borrower did not comply with the Notice of Default then the lender may now issue a Notice of Sale to the borrower, auction houses, and public notices that the property is now foreclosed and will be sold to the highest bidder, usually in cash equivalent.

Notice of Default

Once the borrower has failed to pay the debt (or payments) within the said deadline then the lender will issue a Notice of Default to the debtor. The notice states that the recipient of the letter has not paid their dues in the stated deadline. The letter will also contain a small extension of the deadline for the debtor to pay the obligation.

If the payment is not made within the deadline stated in the notice, then the lender may issue a Notice of Sale to the borrower, the public, or to those connected to the transaction that the property is now foreclosed and is open to a public auction.

A Trustee Sale Guarantee will be requested by the trustee from a title company; the TSG will give assurance to the various liens and encumbrance against the property. The TSG will also contain the parties to receive the Notice of Default.

The 3-months Reinstatement Period

Before the Notice of Sale is issued to the borrower and to the concerned public, a reinstatement period of 3 months is stated by law for the borrower to reinstate the loan. During this period, the borrower may communicate directly with the lender to try to either extend the loan or to pay it in full to avoid a foreclosure.

Notice of Trustee's Sale

During this 21-day publication period, a Notice of Trustee's Sale will be issued indicating the place and time of the actual auction of the foreclosed property. The notice is usually published in the local newspapers or in public notice areas. The Trustees Sale will also contain information about the foreclosed property as anything in it that the trustee wishes to auction off to pay the debt.

After the 21-day period, the property is now eligible to be sold in public. The property will be auctioned off to the highest bidder. But 5 days prior to the date of sale, the borrower may reinstate the loan or postpone the sale if he or she deems it necessary.

Time Frame

It is important to know the time frame for the different processes of a non-judicial foreclosure; this will give you an important edge either in reinstating the loan or trying to catch up with the payment deadline.

The Notice of Default (NOD) will be issued once the maturity date of the loan is reached and the borrower did not pay any of the obligations owed. When the NOD is mailed off to the concerned parties, a 3-month reinstatement period is given as an opportunity for the borrower to renew the mortgage to avoid the foreclosure.

After the reinstatement period, a 21-day publication period of the Notice of Sale is sent off to the newspapers to inform the public of the auction time, date and place. The Trustees Sale will contain all the information of the said auction; this includes the time, place, information on the property and all other assets within it that is auctioned off.

After 5 days prior to the published sale date, the borrower will have another opportunity to reinstate the loan or pay off the remaining debt to avoid the foreclosure of the said property.

Another type of foreclosure is Judicial foreclosure

What is a Judicial Foreclosure?

A judicial foreclosure is quite popular with all lending companies working around the globe. Also called foreclosure by judicial sale, the court will handle all the proceedings of the said foreclosure and make sure that there won't be any more problems for the purchaser of the said property.

Why is judicial foreclosure preferred?

A judicial foreclosure is the preferred procedure simply because all the orders regarding the said property are under the litigation of the court. In other words, every proceeding of the foreclosure are stated and followed according to the statute of law.

Though this type of foreclosure is rather expensive and time consuming since the court will conduct investigation regarding the said foreclosure; the court will also make sure that all the persons connected to the transaction will be duly informed of the said hearing. Most companies would prefer this kind of process since less problems will likely crop up especially to the new owner of the foreclosed property.

When does a judicial foreclosure occur?

Usually, a judicial foreclosure occurs when there is no power of sale between the lender and the borrower in the trust or mortgage deed. When this happens, then the lender will give all the proceedings of the foreclosure to the court and will undergo due process by statute of the state.

How does it work?

In a judicial foreclosure, the court will handle all the proceedings of the foreclosure. The lender will first file a complaint regarding the mortgage to the court, and recording of a List Pending which simply points out to the public that the property is under court litigation and is unfit for sale unless the court releases it from the proceedings.

The complaint will contain details about the debts, the terms and conditions stated in the agreement, and information regarding the security used in the mortgage. The court will review the complaint whether it has sufficient grounds for the property to be foreclosed.

Once the decision is in, that foreclosure is imminent, the court will now inform the concerned parties, this includes the lender, the borrower, or any other persons connected with the said transaction. A notice will be sent to those in question with information regarding the time and place of the hearing for the foreclosure, and the court will provide an opportunity for the borrower to be heard regarding their reason for not satisfying the agreement with the lender.

If the court finds the foreclosure valid, then it will give out a judgment regarding the total amount owed, interest and the cost of the foreclosure process. Once the sale has been made then the court will now distribute the earnings to first satisfy the debt, other concerning parties, costs and finally the borrower.

Sheriffs Sale

After the court finds the foreclosure valid then it will issue a Sheriffs Sale which gives the authority for the foreclosed property to be sold to the public. The notice will be sent out which includes the date and time of the said auction, which can be done anywhere from the court house to any designated areas deemed worthy by the court.

The term of the sale would be auctioning the property to the highest bidder. If the price cannot be paid in full by the buyer, then an initial deposit is required wherein the remaining balance will need to be paid within 30 days after the sale. The Sheriffs sale will be delivered to the new owner of the property as well as the deeds or any documents pertaining to it.

Distribution of the proceeds

The court will make sure that all the parties connected to the foreclosure receive the proper amount due. First, the court will pay off the cost of the judicial foreclosure. This includes the advertising, legal fees of the lender and the auctioneer's fees. The claims of the lender and other parties will also be paid off, with the remainder going to the borrower.

If the price of the property of the auction is less than the actual price stated by the court, then by legal means the court can refuse to ratify the sale to prevent the lender from profiteering from invalid or strategic foreclosures.

If the property is not sold during auction, then the lender will gain full ownership of the property and it will be sold accordingly under their own terms and agreement to pay off the debt owed to them by the borrower.

Chapter 3: Developing a Plan to Stop Foreclosure

Some would see a mortgage loan as an easy way out of a financial crisis, by using their property as security. Yet, irresponsible mortgage management can lead to the foreclosure of your asset, if you are not careful. Here are some tips that you may find useful before your property is taken away from you.

Consult the experts

One piece of advice before applying for a mortgage loan is to consult experts. Most real estate brokers and financial advisers are well informed when it comes to the best deals by different lenders, as well as information about the mortgage itself. They can inform you of the stipulations as written in contracts and will organize them for you; they can inform you of maturity dates, interest rates and also possible ways to extend the deadline to avoid foreclosure.

The financial advisers can analyze your current financial status, as well as the purpose of the loan, and will determine the amount that you may safely borrow from the lender. The real estate brokers can inform you of the best deals in town, since they have numerous contacts with different companies. With these two working hand in hand, they can easily help you to organize your mortgage loan and steps to avoid foreclosure.

Get only what you need, don't overdo it

If you go through the loan without the help of real estate brokers or financial advisers, then you should be careful with the amount that you intend to borrow. It is a common fact that most properties were foreclosed due to irresponsible borrowers who loaned ludicrous amounts of money without being able to pay it back.

Sadly, that is the state of the economy at the time of this writing.

Try to avoid the temptation of going for a large loan. If you are planning to use it to refinance a business or for home improvement purposes then you better analyze your current financial status if you can pay the amount on the maturity date or maintain your payments in a timely manner.

Also, try to scout around for the best deals in town. The internet is a good source of information for various lenders in your area; try to look for a lender with the lowest possible interest rate.

Know the paperwork

One good tip to avoid foreclosure is to know the various paperwork involved in a mortgage. There are two kinds of paperwork that can help you avoid foreclosure of your property: one is the promissory note, and the second is the deed of trust or lien.

A promissory note is usually made by the borrower when they fail to pay the full amount on the maturity date. The note usually contains the request of the borrower from the lender to extend the maturity date of the remaining amount, the maturity date, and remaining unpaid amount and of course, the interest rate. This is quite useful if you don't want your property to be foreclosed for not paying the full amount.

A deed of trust can also be used to avoid foreclosing your property to lenders. A deed of trust acts as a security interest, or a lien, in which the lender may confiscate temporarily the property while the debt is still existent. Once the debt is paid in full, even after the maturity date, the lender will not give back the title of the property back to the borrower.

Always keep in touch with your lender

A very important tip is to always try to keep the lines of communication open between the lender and the borrower. Doing so will not only improve the relationship between the two; it will also help to gain the trust of the lender.

Another practical reason for opening a communication line with the lender is to receive updates regarding the mortgage and foreclosure. By doing so, you will be well informed regarding various stipulations of the mortgage and avoiding foreclosure. Also, they can inform you if the maturity date is coming up so you can plan out in advance how to pay for it.

It is very important for the borrower to pay attention to details when it comes to acquiring a mortgage; not only should you be well informed of the various facets of the contract, the more you know the better the odds of avoiding a possible foreclosure of your property.

Chapter 4: How to Avoid Home Foreclosure

In these tough economic times, more Americans than ever are finding it difficult to pay the home loan notes they signed several years ago, or even more recently. The housing seller's market a few years back gave buyers an ever-increasing confidence in buying real estate as an investment. They watched the price of houses skyrocket and felt that their home's value would never fall and would only increase. Now, many of those same people are looking for advice about how to avoid home foreclosure.

In addition to the rather exorbitant prices many homeowners paid for their houses during the real estate boom that the nation underwent about five years ago or so, the "market value" of their homes was pretty exorbitant also. Many of those homeowners decided to cash in on the value of their homes by taking out second mortgages or lines of equity based on the high values associated with real estate at the time. Now, many of those same people are looking for advice about how to avoid home foreclosure.

So, how do you avoid home foreclosure?

1. Make your mortgage payments every month, even if it means doing without other things. If necessary, eat rice and beans.

2. If you begin to fall behind in your loan payments, do not avoid the lender's calls or letters. That kind of behavior just makes the bank more likely to begin foreclosure because they think you will absolutely never be able to repay your loan and don't even want to try.

3. Put your house up for sale. Getting out from under may be the best way to avoid foreclosure if you are able to sell. Some houses are still selling, even though the selling market is quite slow.

4. Seek the advice of a professional. There are companies and other groups to help you evaluate your situation and perhaps represent you. Some are for profit and some are nonprofit.

5. Understand the language of your original home loan and any subsequent loans you took out on your home. Some mortgages have helpful information about how to avoid home foreclosure attached to, or included in, the mortgage.

6. Contact a housing counselor at Housing and Urban Development (HUD).

7. Make your mortgage payment before any other payments. If you have unsecured debt such as credit cards, pay those only after you have paid your mortgage.

8. Increase your income. You can get a second job or maybe someone else in the family can. If you are always buying your teenage son's clothes, perhaps it is time for him to get flip burgers or stock shelves so he doesn't have to turn to you for every expense.

9. Look into loss mitigation. HUD can help you with this, as can other experienced professionals.
10. Re-negotiate your loan with your lenders. Most lenders want nothing to do with foreclosing on a property and are likely to prefer re-negotiating rather than being forced to foreclose.

If you can follow some of the tips above on "how to avoid home foreclosure" you may well indeed prevent losing your home to foreclosure.

Chapter 5: Foreclosures Are In a Rise; Do Not Ignore the Problem at Hand

Here are several items to take care of as soon as possible.

1. Do not ignore the problem at hand. The further you get behind, the more difficult it will be to bring your loan current and the more likely that you may lose your home.

2. Contact your bank or mortgage company as soon as you know that there may be a problem. Banks or mortgage companies do not want your home. Most of them have options to help you through difficult financial issues.

3. Be sure to Open all correspondents and respond to all mail from your bank, Mortgage Company or lender you are affiliated with. The first notices that you may receive will normally offer good information about preventing foreclosure of your property. If you wait later the mail may include notice of pending legal action against you. If you do not open your mail it will not be an excuse in foreclosure court.

4. Be sure you know your mortgage rights. All mortgage companies are different. Find all of your loan documents and read them so that you will know what your lender may do if you cannot make your payments on time. Learn about the foreclosure laws

in your state and how much time it gives you and your mortgage company to get out of default.

5. Be sure you understand the foreclosure prevention options for your lender. Valuable information about foreclosure prevention options can be found all over the internet just be sure you locate your states local laws.

6. Contact a HUD approved housing counselor that will help you. Your local HUD office will normally fund free or very low cost housing counseling throughout the nation. These counselors can help you understand your options and the laws of your state and organize your finances and represent you in negotiations with your bank if you need their assistance.

7. Spend your money wisely. After your health keeping your house in order should be your first priority. Go over your finances with a fine toothed comb and see where you can change your spending habits and make your mortgage a priority. Look for optional expenses that you can change or even eliminate.

8. Avoid those foreclosure prevention companies; some will take you for a ride. You do not need to pay fees for foreclosure prevention because you can use that money that you would pay them and pay on your mortgage.

You do not have to lose your home.

Taking care of a foreclosure is a like taking care of a cancer. The sooner you catch it, the better chance of survival you may have. Early on in a default process, borrowers can still come back from the lows quicker so the loan company will not have to take too much trying to get you back in line. As the foreclosure process moves along, the harder it is to get your finances back in order. The bank legal costs that customers are usually charged with will grow. If you try to ignore your financial problems and your lenders' phone calls you will likely come closer to losing your home. Lenders are looking to help.

Services should be gone over at every step of the process to try to help you stay in your home. The sooner that there is a connection between the lender and the borrower the easier you will be able to work together. Mortgage companies, banks, and investors do not do this out of the kindness of their hearts. They look better from a public relation standpoint and usually cost thousands of dollars less than full foreclosures. Put yourself in the bank's shoes. If a person has missed one or two payments then you know in your state that you are going to be looking at not getting any payments for up to a year and a half. The wheel starts turning once a borrower becomes 16 days late. The Mortgage Company or bank will try to get in touch with the customer at that point and figure out a way to bring the payment current. After the first payment becomes 30 days late and the next month's payments look to be in jeopardy they will try to collect. In a more serious case, the customer may have already missed two or three payments and owes a couple thousand dollars in lender legal fees. The finance company or bank will still try to arrange a repayment schedule that will work for you and them. Loan modifications go a step further and they are designed for customers that cannot afford repayment plans. In a modification, the financial institution actually adjusts the terms of the loan to make it affordable. It may lengthen the schedule or lower the interest rate to cut the monthly payments, or it may roll the past due amount into the loan and re do the new balance so you can pay the additional debt back over time. If the customer has a more serious financial problem, such as a longer-term job loss followed by rehire at another company that pays much less, there are still alternatives. The financial institution may agree to help the borrower get rid of the house via a pre-foreclosure sale. In more dire circumstances, the servicer will agree to a rapid sale. In these sales, the lender lets the borrower sell the house for less than the outstanding loan amount and the bank will take the proceeds and forgive the remaining overage. Banks are willing to do this because they often lose less on these types of deals rather than going through a foreclosure.

Following the same logic, customers should try to renegotiate the best deal they can get. Someone whose property has fallen in value below the mortgage amount because of a neighborhood decline should consider pushing for a short sale or short refinance rather than a repayment plan. Doing it that way, the borrower doesn't pay any more money than necessary. Regardless of the things you do to get out of foreclosure without racking up extensive legal bills and ruining your credit history, are to start working on a solution before their problems get out of hand and you cannot help yourself get out of the situation at hand.

Chapter 6: Your Foreclosure Options

Are you a homeowner who is facing foreclosure? If so, you may be unsure as to what your options are. Now is the time to find out. Why? Because you may be surprised how many ways there are to avoid foreclosure. When foreclosure is avoided you can either retain your home, keep your credit in good standing, or do both.

When facing foreclosure, the first step you should take is to approach your bank. It is best if you do this before the issue of foreclosure arises. Once it does, it is still not too late to schedule a meeting with the chief loan officer at your bank. If you can prove that you intend to get your mortgage back in good standing or that your financial troubles are only temporary, your lender may hold off on foreclosure.

Even if your lender is willing to work with you, keeping your home may not be in your best interest. If you are having long-term financial hardships, it may be within your best interest to sell your home before it enters into foreclosure. When making this decision, you may want to talk to your lender. They may agree to allow you to proceed with a pre-foreclosure sale. In fact, they may hold off on the process of taking your home, giving you ample time to find a new buyer. When selling your home as a pre-foreclosure, your home can be listed as for sale by owner or through a professional realtor.

Even if you do not consider a pre-foreclosure sale to be an option, you should expect to hear from hopeful buyers. When you are delinquent on your mortgage, especially to the point of foreclosure, this information becomes public knowledge. Some buyers, namely professional investors, seek out those in trouble. Although having a stranger appear at your door or call offering to buy your home may be rude, it is a decision that you may want to give serious thought to.

Another option that you, as a homeowner, has during foreclosure to hire the services of an attorney. When doing so, see those with specialties in foreclosures or real estate. A lawyer can advise you on what steps to take. They can help you understand the pros and cons of pre-foreclosure sales. In some states, attorneys can use bankruptcy as a tactic to stop the foreclosure proceeding. Although not a long-term fix, it may buy you more time to make a decision. It is important to note that bankruptcy, by itself has a whole list of pros and cons.

Most states have what are known as redemption period laws. These are designed to protect homeowners. They give you a grace period to reclaim your home. If you can make good on your mortgage payment, the foreclosure proceedings will stop. States that have these laws often enable you to reclaim your property even after it has been sold at a foreclosure auction. This is provided that you act within the allotted time frame.

If you reside in a state where you are not given a grace period or a redemption period, you always have the option of buying your home again. Anyone can place a bid at a foreclosure auction. With that in mind, placing a bid and being the winning bidder are two different things. It often takes a significant amount of cash to reclaim your home. Your financial lender will also likely attend waiting to pounce. If the bids are not high enough, they will buy your home themselves. This is done to minimize their money lost. Later, your home will be available for sale as a REO (real estate owned) home.

Chapter 7: Foreclosure Can it Be Stopped

Are you a homeowner who has been ignoring the warning letters and telephone calls from your bank? If you are, you may find yourself in the middle of a foreclosure crisis. At this point in time, fear may automatically set in. What will you do? Where you will live? Can you afford to move? Before you let fear take over, it is important to know that foreclosures can be stopped. Although this process is not easy, it can be done.

It is advised that you speak with your financial lender as soon as you find yourself experiencing financial difficulties. For example, when you get laid off or fired from your job, schedule an appointment to meet with your lender and develop a plan, before any problems arise. At the very least, communication should be made when you start receive intent to foreclosure notices. Even if you have a sign on your home stating that the foreclosure process has officially begun, you can still talk to your financial lender. In this instance, the sooner you do so the better.

As for why you should talk to your financial lender, even at the last minute, they want to avoid foreclosure as much as you do. Often times, lenders lose a considerable amount of money on the sale of foreclosure homes. If you can prove that your financial troubles are only temporary, your lender may give you a reprieve. They may stop the foreclosure proceedings for you. As for what can lead to this, you or your spouse getting a second job can help.

If you are dealing with a locally owned and operated bank, which you have been a loyal customer of, it is important to outright ask what can be done. Offer suggestions yourself, if you do not receive them. Could you continue making all future mortgage payments on time, but develop a payment plan for your past due amount? Can you only pay interest for the time being? Can you be given time to sell your home, as opposed to simply just losing it? These are all important questions that you should ask.

Another way that foreclosures can be stopped, in most states, is with a declaration of bankruptcy. However, this step is one that should not be made on a whim. It is first important to meet with an attorney specializing in bankruptcy. If you file for bankruptcy will the foreclosure proceedings stop? Can you make it so that your home is not considered an asset in bankruptcy proceedings? If so, this is the avenue that you may want to take. However, since bankruptcy can negatively influence your credit, it should only be used as a last resort.

Before you take any action with the hopes of stopping foreclosure, you need to closely examine the situation at hand. For starters, would you like to get out from under your property? If it is a money-pit that needs constant repairs, it might just be easier to go the route of foreclosure or even outright allow your bank to sell the property. If you want to keep your home, make sure that you can honestly do so. It is recommended that you take forty percent of your income and apply that towards your living expenses, this includes mortgages and taxes. If this isn't possible for you to do, the avoidance of foreclosure now may result in the process starting again in a few months.

Chapter 8: Foreclosure: How and Why You Should Talk to Your Bank

Are you homeowner who is facing foreclosure? If you are, your first thought may be to start packing. Yes, this is the only choice for some in foreclosure, but that doesn't mean it is yours. Before you throw in the towel, make an appointment in person to speak with your financial lender. You may be surprised how much help, assistance, or advice you may receive when doing so.

First and foremost, it is important to know that banks and other financial lenders are not evil. It may sound silly, but this is how many homeowners feel when facing foreclosure. Many want to know how another human being can force them to leave their own home. In the heat of the moment, many do not realize that banks want to avoid foreclosures just as much as homeowners do. Financial lenders often lose money on foreclosure properties. That is why it is imperative that you schedule an in person meeting with your lender.

As nice as it is to know that you should meet with your financial lender when you feel that you are facing foreclosure or know for sure that it is looming, you may be unsure how to proceed. For starters, many homeowners want to know when the discussion should start. In all honesty, it should start as soon as you know that you will miss a mortgage payment. It is best not to wait until the foreclosure process starts. If you can make payment, but need to do so a few weeks late, be sure to make your actions known. This will prevent your lender from even considering foreclosure right away.

One of the many reasons why homeowners are facing foreclosure is because of the job market. Long-term employees are now finding themselves standing in the unemployment line. If you are laid off from your job, schedule a meeting with your mortgage holder immediately. They may be willing to work with you, provided you will be taking proactive steps to find a new job. Often times, you may find your monthly mortgages payments temporarily reduced.

When your home enters into foreclosure, you will see signs posted on the building. With that said, this is not the first notice that you will receive. As a reminder, banks want to avoid foreclosure just as much as you do. That is why they will likely call and send regular notices to your home. As embarrassing as it may be to admit that you cannot make your mortgage payments, it is important to answer the phone. Remember, your bank may be willing to work with you and create a temporary payment plan. This is often the case when you can prove your financial hardships are only temporary. For example, are you temporarily unable to work due to an injury? Were you laid off, but looking for a new job? If so, make it known.

It is also important to determine how much you need to pay to stop the foreclosure proceedings in their tracks. Since banks want to avoid foreclosure, they may accept a portion of the money that you owe. With that said, this is where you need to proceed with caution. If the bank requires full payment the following month, make sure you can make that payment in full. If not, the process will simply just restart from the beginning all over again.

When discussing your options with your bank, it is important to do so in person. You will want to show your lender that you intend to get back on track financially, but this is difficult to prove over the phone. Walk into the bank with your head held high, dress professional, and be very confident. You need to prove to your lender that the words coming out of your mouth are true. Just because you say you are looking for a new job, it doesn't mean that you are.

Chapter 9: Understanding the Paperwork on Your Mortgage

Many properties, whether residential or business, are slowly disappearing due to foreclosure. The best way to avoid this from happening to you is to understand the documents pertaining to your mortgage loan and foreclosure including the mortgage, promissory note and a deed of trust.

Let's Review - What are Mortgages?

The term mortgage, or mortgage loan as it is normally called, is associated with foreclosure. In a sense, when a loans maturity date is reached without payment of both the principal amount and interest, then foreclosure is imminent for the property.

A mortgage is using a property, whether real estate or commercial, to be used as a security for payment of a debt, or a mortgage loan. Normally, a mortgage loan is used to refinance a business or to be used as a basis for home improvement or for out and out purchase of a home. When done, a contract, or a mortgage, will then be made by the lender containing the information of the said property, the amount loaned and the interest rate incurred by the principal amount, and the maturity date.

When the borrower fails to pay the exact amount as stated in the mortgage, then they may issue a promissory note requesting the lender to extend the maturity date.

Promissory Note and what's in it?

A promissory note is simply defined as a note or a contract which specifies detailed terms regarding the payment of a debt from the borrower to the lender. The note contains the amount owed by the borrower to the lender, the interest rate and the deadline for the payment or maturity date. A promissory note is also very useful for the purpose of tax and record keeping of the said transaction since it is obviously honored as a legal document.

A promissory note is used when the borrower fails to pay the agreed amount on time and requests an extension. If the lender agrees, then the promissory note will become a contract regarding the promised payment, and can be used in any legal proceeding during the time of foreclosure of a judicial sale.

There are two kinds of promissory notes currently being used; one is the normal promissory note which contains the above information, and the demand promissory note which contains the same information as above yet no deadline of payment is stated. One catch of using a demand promissory note is that the lender can demand the payment from borrower at any time they see fit. Normally, the lender will inform the borrower in advance concerning the date of payment.

The concept of a Deed of Trust and a lien

A deed of trust is simply an attached document which serves as a security interest by the borrower to the lender to be able to pay for a certain debt or a loan.

Usually, a deed of trust is considered a lien rather than a stipulation stating a transfer of title of the property from the borrower to the lender.

Also, liens can be considered as non-possessory security interests which grant the lender from holding or securing the said property without resulting in a sale until the debt is paid.

A deed of trust is often used since the cost is less compared to an actual mortgage contract. The deed is a non-judicial document and only contains the agreement between the borrower and the lender. Also, using a deed of trust is much more preferable by the lender since the process of foreclosure can be speed up from 1 year to a mere 3 months.

Keep tabs on anything that's written; If you can't pay the mortgage payment in full by the maturity date then you can initiate a promissory note between you and the lender to extend the time of payment. You may also use a deed of trust or a lien when you don't want your property to be sold during foreclosure, which will give you ample time to get your property back as stipulated in the deed or lien.

In applying for a mortgage loan, it is always important to keep a close eye on your documents pertaining to the transaction; and knowing the importance of each can give you the elbow room that you need to maneuver your property away from foreclosure.

Chapter 10: Re-Negotiating the Loan

The best deals in both mortgage and foreclosure are only through negotiations with your lender. If done just right, you may be able to reduce interest rates, extensions for payment, even extend the maturity date of your debt obligation to avoid foreclosure.

Institutional Lenders

Any company or organization that lends money, either for business or personal reasons, that charges interest fees are called Institutional Lenders. Banks, insurance companies or loan organizations lend money from depositors rather from their own pockets. The loans given out by institutional lenders are regulated by law and must follow certain statutes of the states regarding the release of the said loan.

Negotiating with institution lenders may prove quite difficult since the transaction will be a one-way street; wherein the lender will request various documents from the borrowers and decide if he or she is valid for a loan or not. Not much room is left for negotiations considering these lenders follow very strict guidelines carefully.

Also, institutional lenders will make sure that deals are opened on their end and will try to persuade the borrower that what they are offering is indeed the best deal in town. When you are facing foreclosure and want to steer your property away from it, then your best choice of action would be to visit your lender and tell them what you are facing. If you are having financial troubles then tell them. Make your needs known, just make sure that you sound convincing enough to point out that the loan is risk-free.

Though one possible way of negotiating with institutional lenders is to hire the services of a mortgage broker or a financial adviser; these individuals have multiple contacts with such organizations and they will be able to find bargaining chips to give you the edge on your loan. Also, since they know the statute of the law regarding credit, they will be able to point out options that you might find appealing.

Private Lenders

Private lenders are those who provide loans out of their own pockets and aren't as controlled by strict compliance with the law. It is true that private lenders do follow the basic rules when it comes to loans, since they are working independently rather than organizational, they are open to negotiations as compared to their institutional counterparts.

As with most lenders, these individuals or organizations are keen on the possible risks when it comes to loans. They might request various financial documentation and references from borrowers and analyze each carefully to see if there are low to no risk involved.

For the borrower, this should be an opportunity to negotiate. Try pointing out that your loan is risk free by pointing out hard facts that will reflect on your use of the money. You may also want to keep an eye out on the market for interest rates so that you will be able to negotiate to the point of getting the best deal possible.

If you are facing foreclosure due to an unpaid loan and want to request for an extension then you better inform the lender about it. Try to point out, with documents as proof that you will be able to pay within the extension that you requested.

Pre-plan your negotiations

When dealing with institutional or private lenders, it is also advisable to pre-plan your negotiations carefully so that you can get the best deal when it comes to interest rates or maturity date extensions. This is quite important when you are dealing with imminent foreclosure on your property.

When you want to avoid foreclosure with these lenders, you need to first show them that you can pay them but maybe not at the moment. You need to point out reasons regarding why you can't pay your debt as of yet. A possible reason maybe that you are currently in the process of renovating to improve the sales or income generating factor of your company; try to prepare documentation which screams out the fact that your loans are risk free - Financial statements to support the loan, as well as periodic cash flow to show the lender that your business is productive and guarantees that you can pay them in full at a later date.

This option would allow you to use the equity that you have already established in your home as a way to pay off the delinquent amount in your current mortgage loan. Your monthly payments may even be reduced, but this depends on the interest rate of your new loan.

1. Modifying the Terms of the Loan - An option like this will allow you to refinance the debt in your mortgage, or even to extend the current term of your existing mortgage loan. Modifications are changes that are made to a mortgage loan without having to refinance.

2. Developing a Workout Plan - Developing a repayment plan typically involves establishing a new schedule that allows you to make full regular monthly payment plans to your lender plus a little bit of extra money every month so that you can repay the delinquent amount that you owe over a pre determined amount of time.

3. Forbearance - Special forbearance plan options may give you a temporary reduction or a temporary suspension of your monthly mortgage payments based on the lender's ability to later increase your payments at a point where you are more financially stable. The increase in your payments will cover the delinquent amount that was accrued, but over

a longer period of time than simply demanding payment in full.

There are also options available that allow you to dispose of your home to avoid the foreclosure process all together. While losing your home all together is not always an ideal situation, it is a viable option and therefore is well worth exploring.

In situations where you do not have interest in retaining ownership of your home, the following disposition options may be available to you as alternatives to the foreclosure process. These options will affect your credit rating a lot less than the foreclosure process would.

- Sell the Home - If there is a sufficient amount of equity in the property, you could actually receive more for the property than what is currently due on the mortgage loan, allowing you to pay the mortgage off and to walk away with some cash in your pocket as well.

- Assumption - Using this option, what you would do is to sign the property over to another person who would take over the possession of your home, and would handle making the payments from that moment forward.

- Pre-Foreclosure Sale - This option, which we will touch on more in the next chapter, will allow you to sell your property for less than what is necessary to pay for your mortgage loan.

- Deed in Lieu of Foreclosure - This option may allow you to "give back" the property to your lender voluntarily, without damaging your credit further than you already have.

If you do decide to sell your home, because time is of the essence in the foreclosure process, you need to be quick about it. While you may not necessarily fetch a lot of money for the property, to avoid foreclosure it is important to accept what you are offered in many cases.

Your luck in this situation may lay in the fact that there are many savvy investors out there who are looking to buy properties for decent amounts of money in the pre foreclosure and foreclosure phases. Homes that have been defaulted on still often have equity in them, and this equity can be extremely valuable to the right investors.

If you are having difficulty working with a real estate agent that has what it takes to quickly sell your home, you may want to start looking for investors who pay cash for homes that have been defaulted on or pushed into the pre foreclosure phase.

While it is not a good idea to have to give your home up, in some circumstances the only way to protect yourself from foreclosure is to pay the entire mortgage loan off quickly by unloading your house to the first investor who offers you a good deal. If you wait and the lender takes your home, you will get far less for it than you deserve and may still end up owing money to the lender.

Chapter 11: Can You Get Out of Foreclosure by Refinancing

The foreclosure of a property is one thing that everyone should avoid. There are plenty of ways to save your asset from being foreclosed by your mortgage holder including paying the debt in full or issuing a promissory note so you can extend the deadline, or you can use the method of refinancing.

What is refinancing?

Undertaking another loan to pay off an existing debt is what we call refinancing. In simple terms, most borrowers undergo refinancing to extend the repayment time or to take advantage of reduced interest rates. You can say that refinancing is a secondary loan to pay for the first one. Not only will your property be safe from foreclosure since you are able to pay on time, you also have a form of extension to your debt as well.

But before you go for the idea of refinancing, you first need to know the different kinds of loans and the details before you dive in.

Types of loans

There are two kinds of loans in the world of finance. The first one is the secured loan in which the borrower uses an asset as a pledge or a security as collateral for the loan; this kind of loan is closely regulated by state law and will only be released if the borrower has reached a certain level of criteria from different financial institutions. A good example of a secured loan is a mortgage loan, in which the borrower will approach a lender for credit for purchasing a property or to refinance a business or an existing loan.

Once the borrower fails to pay for the said loan then the lender, or the mortgage holder, will get full right of the property used by the borrower as collateral. The lender will now have the option to sell the property to pay for the debt of the borrower.

The second type of loan is called the unsecured loan, wherein the lender is not governed by the statutes of the state and is not based on the borrower's assets. Unsecured loans come in different forms: credit card debts, bank overdrafts, personal loans from private lenders, credit lines, and corporate bonds.

Interest rates for these two kinds of loans may vary depending on the locale of the financial institution. Since secured loans are governed by legal statute so the interest rates are closely regulated by law; and unlike its counterpart, unsecured loans especially by private lenders are quite known in charging marginally higher interests.

Getting yourself a refinance lender

If you want to find the best refinance lender that will suit your needs then you need to do a lot of research. One way to seek out prospective refinance lenders is through the internet. Most companies, both private and institutional lenders, are now using the Internet to advertise their companies so it's quite easy to seek them out. Try to spend time looking for the lenders with lowest interest rates so that you can get the best deal in refinancing; try not to stick with one since there are countless of lenders out in the World Wide Web that you can work with.

Also, try to look for a lender that has all the fees and costs laid out first hand. Scam lenders often claim good deals without telling the borrower about hidden fees and costs. Honest lenders will give you a draft of possible costs during the transaction.

Closing costs in refinancing

When you have found the right refinance lender, you need to know about the closing costs so you won't be surprised when the lender brings them out for show. Closing costs for a refinance mortgage will include escrow and title fees, lender fees, appraisal fees, insurance, taxes and credit fees.

Though this might sound quite alarming at first; you'll relax once you know what's involved with all these closings costs. Major fees includes the title and escrow fees, but you are usually given a choice to add these fees to the mortgage balance to be paid in full later when it reaches maturity.

The borrower may also aim a no-cost closing method in refinancing. This method is devoid of adding fees but will contain a much higher interest rate than the usual refinance with closing costs. Knowing the cost of your refinance mortgage will not only leave you in the dark when your lender starts talking about fees, but will also give you enough leverage for intense negotiations.

Chapter 12: Are You a Veteran? What is SSCRA and Are You Covered

SSCRA or the Soldier and Sailor Civil Relief Act were signed by President Bush on December 2003. The main point for this act was to set new legislation to simplify or ease both legal and economic burdens to military personnel whether active or retired.

Overview of the SSCRA

The SSCRA addresses the inability of military men to meet financial obligations when they are on active duty. Financial obligations include rentals, leases, mortgages, credit card payments and other similar transactions. The SSCRA also stretches to cover the dependents of the military men in question.

SSCRA covers those under active duty, this includes out on basic training exercise or assigned in the field. Most veterans fail to pay their financial obligations since they are unable to do so during the line of duty. The SSCRA aims to provide legislation to these individuals so that they are given consideration regarding deadlines and maturity dates.

One area covered by SSCRA for military personnel and their dependents includes leasing/renting of a property for residential purpose not more than $1,200 a month. Also the conditions must be met and the transaction must first be made before the service man is enlisted into active duty.

Since they are on active duty, it's almost impossible for them to settle the obligation. On this note, the service man must send a request of being under the protection of the SSCRA to the court when he or she receives an eviction notice. If the judge finds sufficient grounds which merit the protection from SSCRA then the court may postpone the eviction until the term of duty of the personnel expires.

Advantage of SSCRA for veterans on active duty

Most of the military personnel on active duty will not have the ability to fulfill their financial obligations to various institutions like credit cards, banks, insurance or mortgage lenders. The SSCRA aims to provide a form of security to these men on duty for their role in preserving peace and justice in their country.

The SSCRA will provide enough elbow room for the military personnel to be given extended deadlines for payments, foreclosures and mortgage transactions when they are in the line of duty. Though not all veterans are given the privilege of being under the protection of the SSCRA; some criteria and requirements must be met for both the transaction and the personnel before they are granted protection.

SSCRA and Interest Rates

Veterans on active duty who are unable to pay financial obligations such as mortgages and who are facing foreclosure may then invoke the protection of the SSCRA to avoid such problems. Qualified debts are those incurred prior to service men coming into the line of duty. Also, the request will only be valid if the personnel are in the line of duty when the request was made which limited them from settling the said obligation.

When qualified, the service man needs to send a letter to the lender requesting that their interest rate be capped to 6% according to the provision stated in SSCRA. Also, they may need to send a photocopy of the military order to the lender as proof that they are on military duty as stated in their letter of request.

SSCRA and Foreclosures

The SSCRA also covers the military personnel under the obligation of a mortgage, trust deed or security of property for any financial obligation. The SSCRA simply states that the personnel are valid for protection under the SSCRA if the obligation and the property were done prior to their military service.

The provision states that prohibition of foreclosure or sale of mortgage property without the presence of the borrower, the military personnel in this case, whether in a judicial or a non-judicial foreclosure. It is also stated in the SSCRA that maturity dates and deadlines will be given an extension when the military personnel is on active duty until they are released from their given designation.

Even if the maturity date or the date of foreclosure is extended due to the military personnel's inability to pay, the court will try to achieve a compromise agreement from both parties requiring the mortgage lender to pay at least half of the amount due while the mortgage holder extends the deadline or put a stay on the foreclosure or sale of the property.

Chapter 13: How to Use the Court System to Stop a Non-judicial Foreclosure

Non-judicial foreclosure happens without any supervision from the court or any legal statutes in terms of proceedings for foreclosure. Though it might sound as if it's almost impossible for the court system to directly intervene with the proceedings of a non-judicial foreclosure; knowing the details about this kind of foreclosure might give you enough grounds to bring it to legal light.

Non-Judicial Foreclosure: Review

In a non-judicial foreclosure, the lender has the power to impose its authority on the said property once it is foreclosed through the use of the power of sale clause. The mortgage holder, or the lender, will have the ability to make use of the said property to pay off the debt of the borrower by means of a sale or simply putting an embargo on it.

Since there is no legal statute in the transaction between the lender and the borrower, the contract will simply have the essence of authorized in any way the lender might see fit to exercise his or her power over the foreclosed property. In a way, you are simply telling the lender that you are selling the property in advance without any recourse whatsoever.

Check the contract carefully

It is always important for the borrower to read the contract or the agreement carefully before signing a mortgage with a lender; the borrower should take note of clauses and stipulations giving the lender full authority of the property and the like. Take note of the maturity date, interest rates, and hidden fees that the lender might have inserted in the contract.

Grounds to bring non-judicial foreclosure to court

It is true that a non-judicial foreclosure is definitely outside the law since the agreement is between the lender and the borrower, but is also possible for the borrower to bring this foreclosure by power of sale into legal hands.

For the side of the lender, it is almost impossible to bring the matter into court since it's almost impossible to sue a borrower for repayment of the said property. But the borrower may, or may not, have the capability to file for a court hearing even if the foreclosure is non-judicial.

It is important to know the process concerning the foreclosure of a property in non-judicial terms, like the time frame for the issuance of notices to the actual auction of the sale. If the lender has breached certain aspects of the process then you may bring that up to court to file a Temporary Restraining Order (TRO) on the lender to stop the foreclosure or sale of the said property.

If you are not sure if it is possible to bring to court a non-judicial foreclosure then you may need to consult with someone who is knowledgeable about the working of the law when it comes to mortgage and foreclosure. Consulting a lawyer or a financial adviser regarding the state of your foreclosed property and possible grounds to bring to court to enjoin the foreclosure would be your best bet in the situation.

How TRO works

When you have successfully uncovered some grounds to bring the non-judicial foreclosure to court then an issuance of a Temporary Restraining Order (TRO) will be inevitable.

A TRO is a kind of court order stopping the lender from foreclosing the property for a short period of time, usually around 2 weeks or so while the court is conducting a formal hearing on the matter. Under the context of a pending foreclosure, the TRO will enjoin the trustee and the lender from continuing with any non-judicial foreclosure to the property of the borrower until further evidences show the invalidity of the borrower's lawsuit.

Non-Judicial to Judicial

It is true that a non-judicial foreclosure will leave the court out of the transaction, but if the borrower pushes through with the lawsuit when they have sufficient grounds for one will practically turn it into judicial in a blink of an eye.

Since most lenders will opt for a non-judicial foreclosure to save costs in processes and fees that accompanies the said transaction, turning it into a judicial foreclosure will add some more costs to both the borrower and the lender.

Chapter 14: Is Bankruptcy the Answer to Stopping Foreclosure

In most cases in the United States, bankruptcy may be a solution to get a fresh start when the debtor is unable to pay his financial obligations in full. To find out if bankruptcy may be a method to stop a foreclosure, we first need to know about bankruptcy and the different kinds that make it applicable to your situation.

An overview of bankruptcy

In legal terms, bankruptcy is simply defined as the inability of an individual to pay the creditors. Most individuals, who are unable to fulfill their financial obligation to their creditors, or lenders, file for bankruptcy to get a fresh start from their debts. Another definition of bankruptcy is liquidating the assets of the debtor to release them from their liabilities or financial obligations.

There are two kinds of bankruptcy known in any court system. One is the involuntary bankruptcy wherein the lender or the creditor will file the bankruptcy petition against the debtor in court when they are unable to pay off their debts in full. The reason for this is because the lender will simply try to recoup the amount owed to them by the borrower and try get a marginal income from the amount they have somewhat invested to the debtor.

Voluntary bankruptcy on the other hand is when the debtor initiates the petition on their own. One reason for this is the inability of the debtor to pay off the amount owed to the creditor in full, or will try to get out of the financial obligation by declaring in court their state of financially deficiency.

Bankruptcy chapters

There are two kinds of bankruptcy that a debtor can file in court, a Chapter 7 and a Chapter 13 bankruptcy. Each has their own criteria and processes that fit in the situation of the debtor's position.

A Chapter 7 bankruptcy opts for the liquidation of the said property to cover the debt to the creditor. Also, by using this method, the debtor will have some of the proceeds left from the sale of the property to start all over again. The Chapter 13 bankruptcy on the other hand is simply reorganizing the debt in which the creditor will give three to five years for the debtor to pay the amount due.

But be warned that not all debts are covered by bankruptcy; common debts that bankruptcy can be a solution for is credit card debts, unsecured loans and medical bills. It is always best to consult a lawyer or a financial adviser when you plan to use bankruptcy as solution to your problems.

Qualification

Chapter 7 and 13 bankruptcy is not as easy as filing it out directly in court. Each has its own intricacies and qualifications that should fit the situation of the debtor. If you are willing to lose all your assets in settling your debt then liquidation through Chapter 7 bankruptcy would be the best option.

But if the collateral is a business property and the status is booming, then it is best to settle for a Chapter 13. If you are lucky, you may get an approval along with a five year extension to pay off the full, or remaining, amount of your debt.

It has also been noted in the US government that anyone who has already filed a Chapter 7 or Chapter 13 bankruptcy within the last 6 years are not allowed to file the same method again.

If in doubt, consult a professional

When in doubt about choosing bankruptcy as the ultimate solution for your financial woes, then it is best to consult a bankruptcy attorney. These professional can provide insights, as well as suggestions regarding possible solutions to your problems.

If bankruptcy is your final option in the matter, then it is best to consult if a Chapter 7 or 13 bankruptcy would suit you best. There are certain prohibitions in law stating that even if an individual files for a Chapter 7 bankruptcy, it is quite possible to retain some, if not all, of their assets. So consulting a lawyer is your best option if you want to make most out of the situation.

Be aware that bankruptcy laws have changed dramatically in recent years and become much harder to qualify. Your best bet is to consult a professional to get the proper counsel before going this route.

Chapter 15: Should You Sell Your Property to Stop Foreclosure

Trying to get out of a foreclosure situation is a bit too much to handle when you are having financial difficulties. Most often in the United States, most debtors go as far as to declare a bankruptcy in court just to get out from under their debts. But for some, selling their property to stop the foreclosure as well as getting a meager earning for a fresh start can be quite appealing.

Stopping a foreclosure

Before you aim at selling your property to stop its imminent foreclosure, there are other options available before you lose it entirely. One way to pay your debt is to meet with your lender and request a Forbearance. This method is simply defined when a lender will waive some fees on your debt so that you will be able to pay on time.

A debtor can also use refinancing as a method in paying your debt to avoid a foreclosure. You can search around for a lender which provides the best deals in refinancing loans so you will be able to pay your first loan and breathe a little easier with the extended deadline of the second.

Loan modification can also be an option to stop a foreclosure. A loan modification is somewhat akin to refinancing wherein the only difference is that your original lender will grant you a new loan to pay off the first one without re-applying.

Should you sell?

If all these option fail, then the only solution left is to sell off your property to make ends meet with your debts. If you can find a seller before the foreclosing date comes then you will be able to finish paying off your debt without going through the foreclosure process.

A short sale occurs when the creditor, or the mortgage holder, will approve the sale of the property for the total market value. Lenders actually prefer a short sale rather than foreclosure since the cost of the latter is alarmingly high. And, since most lending organizations are in the money business, they would prefer a cash equivalent as payment rather than a property.

Also, this method is quite popular because if done right, you will be able to pay off your debt in full while keeping some of the profit to make a fresh start. But be warned that this method is also quite popular to those who seek to use your financial crisis for their own advantage to make a quick profit.

Where to start?

Before you plan to sell off your property, it's always best to know the playing field before you start the game. You first need to consult a real estate agent to know the actual value of your property. It's safe to say that if you consult a professional firsthand about the market value of your asset then you won't fall prey to foreclosure scammers who prowl around for an easy profit.

Also, before you arrive at a set price for your property, you first need to take a closer look to how much you need to pay your creditor which might include the principal amount, interest rates, and others costs incurred by the transaction. With a specific number in hand, you will be able to find a market value for your home which will not only pay your debt in full; it will also give you enough elbow room to start over.

The process

In case a short sale is chosen rather than a foreclosure, here are some processes that the borrower's agent might need to make in order for the sale to push through. First off, an Authorization to Release Information must be made by the agent on behalf of the seller (debtor) regarding the approval of the sale. If a buyer is already at hand then a Purchase Contract must be made with full signatories from all parties.

A Financial Statement and a Sellers Net Sheet must be prepared by the agent to reflect the total proceeds of the sale of the property. And finally, a Hardship Letter and Documentation must be made by the seller (debtor) to explain the reason of the sale of the said property.

Chapter 16: Deed in Lieu of Foreclosure

A deed in lieu of foreclosure is an instrument or document wherein the borrower will convey all the interests in the property used as collateral in a mortgage loan to the lender or creditor. One reason for this method is to avoid a foreclosure proceeding which is damaging to the image of the borrower and expense of the lender.

Advantage to the borrower

To everyone, a deed in lieu of foreclosure might look disadvantageous to the borrower but in truth it is not. The deed is quite advantageous to both the debtor and the lender and is mostly practiced in any proceedings prior to foreclosure.

One advantage to the borrower is that the deed will automatically release him or her from their debt to the lender; this will include most of the costs that is attributed to the loan. In other words, your debt will be forgiven giving you the freedom from financial burdens when it comes to your loan, even if your property is lost in the process. Even if the deed poses a negative feedback to your credit rating, it is still less harmful than going into a mortgage foreclosure.

It is true that the deed in lieu of foreclosure will not save the property that the borrower used as collateral for the loan; the act in itself will give you another opportunity to strike another mortgage loan if needed. Avoidance with the processes which is attributed to a foreclosure is a definite advantage to both the borrower and the lender.

Advantage to the lender

An advantage to the lender is the total repossession time of the property is considerably less compared to a foreclosure. Also the advantage to the cost of the repossession as well as the cost of the foreclosure proceedings is quite appealing to the lender since they won't need to pay a lot of money to get the property from the borrower.

How to prepare the deed in lieu of foreclosure

First of all, the deed must be made in good faith by both the lender and the borrower, and both sides must go into the transaction voluntarily. Before the deed is made, there must be an agreement between both parties that the property in question is at least equal to the current market value. In most cases, the lender will avoid or junk a proposal for a deed in lieu of foreclosure if the current market value of the property exceeds the total amount owed by the borrower to the lender.

As with most documents pertaining to avoid foreclosure, the deed must be made by the borrower and presented to the lender for approval. The document, or proposal, must state that the borrower pursues the deed voluntarily. This will give the lender the evidence rule in which it will protect the lender from future claims that they have acted on bad faith on the deed in lieu of foreclosure.

It is also important that the deed should have no other liens attached to it since this has been both regulated and followed by law, as well as lending organization in the business.

Also, the lender might request for the property to be vacant and uninhabited while the deed is in negotiations; also, the lender or the mortgage company might request an appraisal of the property in question before the deed is approved. The deed must be made in a minimum of 60 days prior to the date of the foreclosure sale.

Negotiations in the deed in lieu of foreclosure

It is always important to undergo strategic negotiations with the lender when it comes to deed in lieu of foreclosure. More often than not, the deed must contain enough clauses to make it advantageous for the lender while giving the borrower enough elbow room to get the best deal in the bargain since the deal is not possible without the approval of the lender.

Another safe bit of advice for borrowers who plan for a deed in lieu of foreclosure is to get help from a professional, in this case an attorney. These professionals are able to pen the said deed in a way that it will reflect the statutes of law as well as the advantages to both parties.

Chapter 17: Should You Use Professional Help during Foreclosure

When facing imminent foreclosure due to unpaid debts to your creditors, then it is a good time as any to seek the help of professional who can help you stop the foreclosure on your assets.

Real Estate Lawyers

Considering the business that is attributed to mortgage and foreclosure, we can safely say that there's a battalion of professionals that can easily get you out of a tough situation when facing foreclosure. Though their fields of expertise might vary, they still aim for the same goal which is to help you in solving your problems. One such category of professionals is Real Estate Lawyers.

These individuals are well versed when it comes to real estate laws, foreclosures and mortgages of real estate, as well as buyers, rentals and sellers of real estate properties. These lawyers represent the interest of the debtor, borrower or mortgagor, when it comes to dealing with possible foreclosure on their immovable property. Real estate lawyers are well versed when it comes to various intricacies of the statutes of law when it comes to foreclosure on real estate.

They can provide legal counsel on what possible solutions there are to protect your property from foreclosure; and the ability to communicate directly with the lender and negotiate on possible agreements that will save your property while maintaining the best interest of both the mortgage company and yourself.

Despite actions taken by the borrower which will result in the decision to sell off the property to pay off the debts, real estate lawyers can help you with the process of the sale as well as providing information on market values regarding the said property.

Foreclosure consultants

When facing imminent foreclosure from a mortgage company, it is always good advice to visit a foreclosure consultant. These professionals specialize in foreclosure scenarios and are quite knowledgeable in looking for ways to avoid the situation.

Foreclosure consultants have the fore knowledge in stopping or postponing a foreclosure sale by the mortgage company. A way of assisting you is obtaining forbearance from any creditor or mortgagee and can help you exercise the right of reinstatement. They can also help you out by extending your deadline or maturity date to avoid foreclosure on your property and make the payments easier.

These professionals can also provide assistance in applying for a promissory note, acceleration contracts secured by deed of trust or mortgage. They can also help you out by obtaining advance loan or funds from other sources to help you in your payment. Using their contacts to various lenders in the country, they can give you advice regarding which company is open for refinancing as well as the best deals in the process.

Since the borrower's or debtor's credit is on the line, they can help you out when your credit is being impaired due to the notice of default or the conduct of the foreclosure sale issued by the court in request of the lender or the mortgage company.

Do it on your own

It is quite true that hiring professionals like real estate lawyers and foreclosure consultants to help you out with your financial problem might prove costly but considering their line of work and expertise, they are there to help you solve your foreclosure problems.

But if you are on the thrifty side and decide to learn about all the intricacies of the problem on your own to save on the extra cost of hiring these professionals then it could prove to be a daunting task, but not impossible.

The Internet is a good source of information regarding foreclosure and mortgage. Some sites offer tips on how to avoid a foreclosure while some offer definite solutions to get rid of it entirely. Though finding the right site with the perfect information could be painstakingly difficult, you can find the right one with a little determination and patience.

Another way to research foreclosure is to visit forums about it and ask different users their views on the matter. Not only will they be able to provide first-hand experience on their dealings with foreclosure, they might provide you with in-depth information on how to deal with it; all-in-all you might be able to find the perfect solution for your needs.

Chapter 18: Foreclosure Scams

There are predators out there who look at homeowners in poor financial situations as easy prey, devising a number of scams and fraud attempts to take advantage of people who are already on a heck of a financial rollercoaster. It is important that you protect yourself by staying current on the foreclosure fraud and scams that are circulating, so that you do not get taken by one of these fraudsters. Here are some of the more prevalent scams that people are trying to pull over on homeowners and families buying homes or facing foreclosure.

- Sales Leaseback - People often tout this as an easy deal, requiring that the homeowner hand his or her deed over to an "investor" for little or no money, on the basis that the homeowner can continue to live in the home, leasing it back with the option of repurchasing within a year. This may sound like an excellent concept, but there is a serious catch involved.

Even if you sign the deed over to someone else, you are still legally responsible for the mortgage, meaning that you would be paying both the original mortgage and the lease amount to the investor. Paying twice what you were already having difficulty paying will be close to impossible and one missed or late payment will have you evicted from the home, and the home sold out from under you.

- Predatory Lending - Unfortunately, there are a large number of lenders out there who offer loans with the specific intention of taking advantage of borrowers who cannot afford to make the payments. If there is any equity in the home at all, these lenders will attempt to take it all in the form of incredible fees, exorbitant interest rates, and nightmare prepayment penalties. While new laws are being passed that prohibit many of these predatory practices from occurring, it is still quite easy for lenders to take advantage of homeowners in bad financial situations.

Here are some of the predatory lending practices that you need to steer clear of:

1. Frequent Refinancing - The frequent refinancing of loans without offering any real benefits to the homeowner or borrower, or frequent refinancing of loans simply so that the lender may generate additional fees for him or herself.

2. Equity Switching - Equity stripping, by persuading an owner in dire financial straits to take out a loan far beyond his or her ability to repay it.

3. Bait and Switch - Attempts at bait and switch, where lenders advertise a specific set of 'teaser' fees and interest rates, then the rates and fees skyrocket suddenly at the point of closing, reaching points that are beyond the homeowner's means.

4. Appraisal Inflation - Inflating appraisals up front, forcing the homeowner to take on much larger loans with much higher interest rates.

Homeowners lose the opportunity to refinance the amount of the loan at a later time, because the value of the home is no longer enough to cover the full amount of the loan.

5. Loss Mitigation - This practice is regularly referred to as "I can prevent your foreclosure, but only if you pay a fee". People who try to force this type of a process on unsuspecting people tout it as the ability to stop or prevent foreclosure, but only for a fee paid up front. The problem with this type of service is that the "rescuer" cannot guarantee that they will actually prevent your foreclosure from occurring, yet they still collect your fee up front. If you want to protect yourself as a homeowner in a bad financial situation, there are much easier ways to do it without paying exorbitant fees to "rescuers" who more than likely will not be able to help you.

6. List and Sell - This is a scheme that is becoming quite popular among real estate agents and brokers looking for additional income streams. The concept is simple: The real estate agent convinces a homeowner in default to allow the agent to list the home in an attempt to sell it. The real estate agent promises that if the home is not sold within the period before the foreclosure auction, which is typically around sixty days away, he or she will purchase it.

But here is the catch: In too many cases, the real estate agent will drastically overprice the property when listing it in the MLS or Multiple Listing Service, so that nobody expresses any interest in purchasing it. Then when it does not sell, the agent is able to purchase it for substantially less than what it was listed for.

7. Hiding things in the contract - Some scammers and predatory lenders like to hide a variety of different bombshells right in the contract where they cannot be found. They wait until the absolute last minute, and then make these hidden terms known. By now, it is too late for the homeowner to renegotiate the contract, and he or she is trapped dealing with the true intentions of the contract.

Homeowners who are caught in situations like these are very rarely capable of seeking legal advice. They suddenly find out that there are costs behind their resources, but if they fight the contract at closing they could potentially lose their home in the foreclosure process.

There are a number of organizations, like ACORN or the Association of Community Organizations for Reform Now, the Consumer's Union, and the United States Office of Housing and Urban Development or HUD that offer extremely vital and valuable insight into protecting yourself from predatory lending practices and everything that is well within your power to combat these dangerous practices.

Chapter 19: Protect yourself from Foreclosure

As we mentioned before, all is not lost when it comes to protecting yourself from foreclosure. Here are the steps that you need to follow to protect yourself from the foreclosure process. Keep in mind that once your lender has expressed his or her plans to foreclose on your home, your time is extremely limited. This is a fast moving process, and because time is of the essence, you have to act fast if you want to succeed.

1 - For starters, do not ignore the problem. As you become further and further behind in your finances, the more difficult it will become for you to reinstate your mortgage loan. The harder it becomes to reinstate your mortgage loan, the more easily your lender will find it to take your home from you.

2 - Contact your lender as soon as you know that there is a problem. Nothing dictates that you have to wait until your lender plans to foreclose. In reality, lenders do not want your home; they would rather you simply paid your mortgage on time so that they can be paid back for their investment. Because of this, most lenders offer options to help borrowers through a number of different financial difficulties.

3 – As I have mentioned in previous chapters keep in touch with your lender in every step of the process. Open and respond to any and all mail from your lender, because the first notices that you receive will

offer a lot of vital information regarding the foreclosure prevention process. By failing to keep in touch and to open the mail that your lender sends simply will not be a good enough excuse when you finally end up in foreclosure court.

4 - Know your rights and your options when it comes to foreclosure. You can find a lot of valuable information relating to foreclosure prevention or loss mitigation online. Make sure that you know your rights, as informed decision making is the best way to prepare yourself for this challenging process.

5 - Use your assets to the best of your ability. Do you have assets like jewelry, a second vehicle, a whole life insurance policy, or other types of assets that you can sell for cash? Selling items that you can bear to part with will allow you to reinstate your loan. Using your assets to the best of your ability can have a huge impact on your ability to repay your mortgage and to save your home.

6 - Avoid companies that charge money to do what you can do yourself. You should never have to pay exorbitant fees for help with foreclosure prevention. Use that money to pay your mortgage off instead. For profit companies will contact you with a variety of wild claims regarding negotiating with your lender, but they are doing this hoping that you do not realize that you can negotiate with your lender all on your own without their help and overpriced services.

These may be legitimate companies, but there is nothing that they do that you cannot do yourself, and your lender would more than likely rather hear from you than a professional company when it comes to *your* mortgage loan.

There are a variety of options available to you that do not require you to lose your home. With so many alternatives, it seems ludicrous that so many people find themselves losing their properties to a completely avoidable foreclosure.

Chapter 20: Pre Foreclosure

The pre foreclosure period is the period that exists from the day that your lender notifies you of his or her intention to foreclosure, and the date that is set for the public sale of your home. There are a couple of different options available for you to explore at this point, one of which is to pursue a short sale, one of which is a Deed in Lieu of foreclosure opportunity, and the final of which is to talk to someone regarding bankruptcy proceedings.

All three of these situations fit certain circumstances and situations, and not every will qualify. Find out more information about these strategies to see if any of the three is right for your unique circumstances.

- Short Selling - When it comes to real estate, a short sale occurs when the outstanding obligations against a property have become greater than what the property is capable of selling for. The short sale process is a way that homeowners can avoid having their homes foreclosed upon while still paying their loan off by settling with the mortgage lender.

The first step is to verify what the value is for your property, through a real estate broker or through your own market analysis of your property and the surrounding area. Next you will add up all of the costs associated with selling the property, and the amount that is owed against the property which will be the total of all of the loans currently against the property. You will need to do some calculating, subtracting the total amount owed against the property from the estimated sale proceeds. On a short sale, the number that you come up with will be a negative one.

Your next step is to directly contact each lender, talking to someone in the customer service department and explaining the situation to them in detail. They may either recommend you talk to a specific department, or they may put you in touch with the right supervisor or manager right away. The more authority this person has, the better.

Talk to your lender at this point to find out more about what is required for a short sale. Most but not all lenders will be more than willing to work with you, reducing how much money is left on your loan, or making other arrangements for you to follow.

Keep in mind that closing costs tend to include both title and escrow fees, and you may be responsible for these as the seller of the property but it depends on your county. You may also have to deal with notary fees, re-conveyance fees, documentary fees, transfer fees, delivery fees, unpaid property taxes and attorney fees as well.

You also need to keep in mind if you do not use the assistance of a real estate broker when you sell the home, you can save the commission amount and apply it toward your loan instead. But if you feel more secure having a real estate broker, you should consider working with a discount broker who can market your property more cheaply.

- Deed in Lieu of Foreclosure - This is a deed instrument that allows the borrower to convey all of the interest in a piece of real estate property to the lender as a means of satisfying the loan in default and avoiding foreclosure proceedings in the process. This specific process offers a number of advantages both to the lender and to the borrower.

The principal advantage offered to the borrower is that he or she is immediately released from most or all of the debt associated with the loan that has been defaulted on. The borrower is also able to avoid the public notoriety that comes with a formal foreclosure. The lender can enjoy a large reduction in the amount of time and cost that would normally be associated with a home repossession; along with other advantages should the borrower subsequently file for bankruptcy proceedings.

In order for a borrower to even be considered for a deed in lieu of foreclosure, the amount of debt must be secured by the transfer of the real estate. Both parties in the transaction must enter in to the agreement in good faith and voluntarily. What this does, is it enacts the parole evidence rule, protecting the lender from subsequent claims that he or she acted in bad faith or otherwise pressured the borrower into this type of settlement.

Chapter 21: The Pros and Cons of Pre-Foreclosure Sales

Are you a homeowner who is facing foreclosure? If so, know that just because foreclosure is down the road, it doesn't mean that you have to travel that far. You should know that you do have a number of different options. One of those options starts in the pre-foreclosure stages and is known as a pre-foreclosure sale.

As previously stated, not all homeowners are able to receive assistance from their lender. If you find yourself in this position, a pre-foreclosure sale may be the only way to keep your credit in good standing. A foreclosure can negatively impact your credit for years to come. In keeping with credit, some lawyers will have their clients declare bankruptcy to stop foreclosure or hang onto the home. This is also risky.

If you make the decision to sell your home, it is wise to make arrangements with your lender. A financial lender who knows that you are actively trying to sell your home is more likely to give you time to allow that sale to take place. As for that sale, it can be handled by you or by a realtor. If you are upset about the loss of your home, a realtor is advised. This is because it can be difficult dealing with prospective buyers who seem to have no regard for you or your troubles.

If you use the services of a realtor to help with the sale of your home, you may receive more money. This is because retailers tend to sell homes at or around their assessment value. Although not much may be left over, after paying your mortgage and the realtor, it may be enough to help you make new living arrangements. Since buying a home likely isn't an option, you should have enough for a security deposit and first and last month's rent.

As it was previously stated, buyers interested in pre-foreclosure sales aren't always careful with the words they choose. You may have to deal with people who look down on you. Yes, they are usually in the wrong, but you must handle the situation calmly. Unfortunately, there are many misconceptions that surround those facing foreclosure, most of which are not true. Remember to always keep your head held high. As painful as it may be to deal with a "jerk," at least you can avoid foreclosure and keep your credit in good standing.

Perhaps, the biggest downside to selling your home, through a pre-foreclosure sale, is the loss of your home. In fact, this is why many homeowners wait until the last minute to okay the sale of their home. It is a decision that many homeowners are uncertain about. Please know that unless you can get your mortgage back to good standing, you will lose your home regardless. A pre-foreclosure sale at least lets you retain a decent credit score, as your mortgage will be paid off and hopefully in full.

Chapter 22: Surviving a Foreclosure

As long as you are willing to be open and honest with your lender, and you are not afraid to set up some kind of payment arrangement that you can actually commit to; the odds are that your lender will be willing to work with you, allowing you to avoid the foreclosure process all together. If you want to stop or overturn the foreclosure process, something has to be legitimately wrong with the process, and this is not simple.

So instead of simply fighting off foreclosure, you can prevent it completely by making the right monthly payments every month. As I mentioned, there are plenty of alternative options to try if you want to put off the foreclosure process or to stop it all together.

If the sale of your home does take place, try not to fret. You probably still have time to move on to another home before the paperwork has been completely finalized.

When your credit is severely damaged already and then you are forced into the foreclosure process, you will find it even more difficulty to avoid this from happening, especially if you simply do not have the resources necessary to completely avoid a foreclosure. You may not be able to see into the future, but any precautions that you can take to avoid the foreclosure process should be taken as soon as possible.

Foreclosures are occurring at truly record rates, and families and home owners are constantly facing obstacles forcing them to forfeit their ability to make payments on their property mortgages.

After you receive a foreclosure notification, you should call your lender immediately and set up an appointment where you can meet with them in person. Sit down with them individually and try to find out if there is anything that you can do to stop the foreclosure process from occurring. There are new laws that require that credit counseling be offered to debtors from approved non-profit credit advisory companies, hoping to drastically decrease how many people are experiencing foreclosures every year.

As long as you do not owe more money than what your home will sell for in the current real estate market, then selling your home may even give you the profit that you are looking for before your home goes into foreclosure. The key here is to thoroughly explore your options.

You absolutely need to be prepared if you want to survive foreclosure. Try everything that you can first to prevent it from occurring, but know that if you cannot prevent foreclosure, it is not the end of the world. Talk to your lender through every step of the process and see what he or she can do for you as you go along through step by step. Your lender may be able to help you a lot more than you realize.

Chapter 23: Restore Credit Following Foreclosure

It is a common fact that after a foreclosure of your property or filing a bankruptcy to erase your debt from history might give you a negative rating on your credit, it is also good since you will be in the process of starting over. Given that you can start again from zero, you will be able to clean up your act and work your way up again in good financial health.

Before you can start restoring your credit, you need to make sure that you have the mindset for it. You need to remind yourself constantly why you are doing this in the first place; try to remind yourself of the various errors that you made in the past that led to the downfall of your credit rating.

Don't leave your bills unattended

When restoring your credit rating, it's always important to take note of all the transactions that you incurred before and after your foreclosure and bankruptcy incident. Take note of all the transactions which give you a minus credit rating and try to find ways of getting rid of them. If it is an outstanding payment, then you have to make sure that you pay it slow so that it won't burden you financially.

Get your credit record and start cleaning?

Seeing all those negative remarks on our credit reports is simply too much for us to handle. After a foreclosure or a bankruptcy, you should avoid the small problems that add up to a negative credit rating. Here are some tips to get the green back in your credit:

1. Since you are starting again from scratch, try to keep payments on time to avoid messing up your credit even more. Double check all your bills, especially the dates, and make sure that you pay them on time.

2. Try to keep questionable items off your credit report. Keep a close eye on transaction dates, companies, amounts, as well as contact information to determine if you made the transaction or not. If not, then don't ignore it and contact the concerned authorities immediately and have it removed.

3. Steer away from payments with high interest rates. Most of us buy what we want without taking into consideration the interest that is included with the purchases. Even if these purchases might look small at first, it might skyrocket into debt if left unchecked.

Check anyone?

By being part of a foreclosure or bankruptcy, you are showing information to concerned individuals that you were suffering from financial instability. If you are paying in cash or credit for most of your transactions, then you'd better consider paying with check in the near future. Having to pay with a check shows that you have a good financial status with banks and underwriters will be checking these out especially when you apply for a loan.

Horde receipts

Not all payments will be reflected on your credit report immediately; some will take time to update and may show up after a year or two. An example of these non-traditional trade references are cell phone bills, store credit accounts, car insurance payments and other receipts. Try to keep all these transaction records safe since these documents can help you out when you want to show the bank that you are a good credit risk.

Try to gather at least a 'worth of these transaction records and try to file them. When you try to apply for a mortgage loan at a bank or any lending institution then these will come in handy. Just make sure that you paid on time as reflected in the transaction receipt.

A new view on credit cards If you are trying to fix your credit rating for the better then it is a good idea to apply for a secured credit card. These kinds of credit cards allow you to deposit into an account which you can borrow through transactions made with it. By using this kind of method, you are establishing a positive payment history with the bank and in time they might grant you an increased credit line which is greater than your initial deposit.

Losing your home is one of the absolute worst things that can ever happen to most people. Foreclosure is an ugly word, and most people do not want to think about it. What most people do not know, or refuse to believe is that you can recover after a foreclosure, and the sooner you start working at it, the better off you will be.

You simply have to know what to do and how to do it to protect yourself and to begin building your credit back up again. Rebuilding your credit after you have experienced a foreclosure can be a tricky proposition. These are other simple step by step formula for restoring your credit after you lose your home in the foreclosure process.

Step 1 - First thing you need to do is to understand why you were foreclosed on. This is an absolutely vital and extremely important factor in repairing your credit following a foreclosure. Were there circumstances that you could have avoided? If so, you need to understand what they were so that in the future, you can fix them or avoid them all together. If it was simply a series of unfortunately accidents and circumstances beyond your control, do what you can to prevent them from reoccurring.

Step 2 - The next step in the process is to look into how you spend your money. Your personal spending habits may need to see some change so that you can avoid having this same type of problem again in the future.

You need to create a personal budget for yourself, and you need to stick to it at all costs so that you can correct the bad ways that you spend your money. Your goal here is to save some money so that you can better avoid falling into such a negative situation ever again.

Step 3 - Your next step in this process is to pay off all of your debts. This is not going to be an easy task for most people, not by any means, especially if you have a number of different debts to pay off.

However, there are a number of innovative debt consolidation services that are well worth you considering. Just make sure that you do your research and really check out your options because not all debt consolidation companies are created equally, and some companies are fraudulent.

Step 4 - Now your job is to maintain your spending habits. It can be fairly easy for people to fall back into their old habits, the same habits that got them into the foreclosure mess to begin with. Because of this, it is imperative that you be committed to the act of changing.

One of the best ways to make sure that this happens is to cut up your credit cards, this way you cannot be tempted to use them again, especially in the worst possible situations. Getting into debt simply to pay off other debt is absolutely NOT the way that you should handle things.

Step 5 - The final step to build your credit up again after a foreclosure is to make sure that from this point on, you pay everything off on time. This will help you repair your credit step by step after your foreclosure. You need to be willing to make sacrifices if you want to get your bills paid up on time. The more that you show that you have changed, the more quickly you will be able to repair your credit.

Chapter 24 How to Buy Another Home After a Foreclosure or Bankruptcy

Some might think it's impossible to acquire another loan after a bout of foreclosure or bankruptcy. On the contrary, some lending companies do provide mortgage loans to those who have a history with financial difficulties. Even with damaged credit, it is still possible to get a loan and your dream home, and here's how.

It is recommended to forgo getting a loan within a span of 2 to 3 years. These times will be well spent in repairing your damaged credit rating, and will allow you ample time to start over again from scratch.

Fix the problem

Your main problem in applying for a loan after foreclosure and bankruptcy is your damaged credit rating. The first order of business before setting out for a new loan is to restore your damaged credit. Here are some steps on how to restore your negative credit rating:

1. Try to get a credit report and check out each item carefully. Take note of those transactions which give you a negative credit rating. If the negative credit stems from payment problems, then you better concentrate on timely payments. This might take some time depending on the number of transactions

you made with late payments, but everything will all add up in the long run.

2. It is quite possible to obtain a loan even after foreclosure and bankruptcy issues; it is true that it's impossible to get low interests rates from lending companies on the first hand; but as you continue to do on-time payments then you are well on your way to repairing your damaged credit. If the company notices that you've been making on-time payment on a regular basis then they might award you by lowering your interest rates.

3. Getting a new and secured credit card is a good way to improve your credit rating. Try to make on time payments with your new credit card for a year to show the lending organization that you are financially stable and your past woes are now erased from history.

Finding a lender for your new home

It will be difficult to find a new mortgage lender that will provide you with the best deals for your dream home, but never impossible. It is true that your past bout with foreclosure and bankruptcy damaged your credit thus earning you higher interest rates than normal from lenders around your area.

There are two ways to go for a loan even with a damaged credit: one, you can scout around for lenders with manageable interest rates and continually pay on-time so that they can lower the interest rates with your timely payments. Second, you can scout around for various lenders who are willing to give people with bad credit another chance.

Surfing the internet is a great way to find a lender that will suit your needs. Online mortgage brokers will go out of their way to help you out even if you have a damaged credit record. Also, some online lending companies give low interest rates even to ones with bad credit record; try to keep an eye out for these sites since you can get back to them later to compare terms and agreements, conditions and interest rates.

If traditional lenders fail

More often than not, traditional lenders will refuse to do business with people with bad credit records, especially those who just came out of foreclosure and bankruptcy; then the only option you have is through sub-prime mortgage loan lenders.

Even with bad credit, sub-prime and high-risk mortgage lenders do business with people who have credit ratings of 650 and below. The standard score for any traditional lender is 660 and above. Often time, traditional lenders will even raise the requirement to 670 just to be sure that the risk is less when giving out the loan.

Sub-prime and high-risk mortgage lenders are usually found online with sites detailed with various information like requirements, qualification criteria and other services. You would do well to search online for various companies that offer these services to people with damaged credit records.

Chapter 25: Foreclosure Home Maintenance

Homes are most people's biggest investment, and it makes sense to take proper care of them right from the start. Most people do their best to keep up with home maintenance to make their daily living better and more enjoyable as well as protect the investment they made in their home. Even so, there is always something that needs to be done on a house. People who are facing foreclosure generally have fewer resources to spend on home maintenance, so, usually; houses in foreclosure need home maintenance even more so than other houses do.

In addition to the minor repairs that most houses need, foreclosure home maintenance may include repairs that go beyond the typical handyman-special repairs that are a normal part of owning, buying, or selling a home.

Just about any home, foreclosure home or otherwise is going to have some or all of these common home repair needs:
1. Holes in walls – it is quite common to see small holes in drywall. If there are any in your home, they should be fixed.
2. Cracks – lots of homes have cracks in the sidewalks or on walls or on floor or bathroom tiles. Those are hardly even noticeable when you live with them day in and day out, but

others who are looking to purchase a home notice things like that immediately.
3. Leaks – If your kitchen or bathroom faucets leak, they should be repaired.
4. Improperly fitted doors – Sometimes the doors of kitchen cabinets or
5. Bathroom vanities don't close exactly correctly. Usually, replacing a hinge will do the trick.

If you intend to invest in an REO (Real Estate Owned) property, you are almost certainly guaranteed to be taking on foreclosure home maintenance. The above minor repairs are likely to be a part of the package, and you also may face more major repairs. Foreclosure home maintenance needs often include:
1. Roof repair
2. Foundation repair
3. Major appliance repair or replacement
4. Window replacement
5. Wood rot replacement

Even though the thought of having to do major repairs may seem daunting, the price of foreclosed property may make the investment in foreclosure home repair worth the cost and effort. Of course, you should be cautious and seek professional advice before buying any property, foreclosed or otherwise or in need of repair or not.

When you do become a homeowner, whether you purchase an REO (Real Estate Owned) property or make a more traditional purchase, you should always keep your home's value as high as possible by keeping up with repairs and maintenance, but since the whole reason behind foreclosures is financial, you should expect your foreclosure home purchase to come with a list of foreclosure home maintenance issues.

Chapter 26: Your Options As a Renter

Are you a renter who is concerned with foreclosure? With the recent media attention it has received, you may be and with good reason. Although many renters are blindsided by a foreclosure eviction notice, others may have seen the signs coming. Whichever side of the fence you are on, it is important to know what your options are.

One of the most common decisions made by renters who have either been served with a foreclosure notice or see it coming is to throw in the towel and move. Many decide this is the safest and easiest approach to take. With that said, know that you may face a number of obstacles. Unless your landlord has received a foreclosure notice, they do not need to let you out of your lease. If this happens, you legally need to continue paying rent.

Next, you may find it difficult or impossible to retrieve your security deposit. This may be a problem if you weren't anticipating to move, as you may not have the funds needed to pay a new security deposit on a new property. This doesn't mean that you will be left homeless or put out on the street. Remember that you don't have to move until you receive a legal eviction notice. Next, talk to prospective landlords about your situation. If your current landlord can vouch that you do make on time payments, you may be able to make your security deposit in affordable installments.

As previously stated, you do not legally have to move from your rental unit until you have received an eviction notice. For that reason, many renters, especially those who were unprepared, make the decision to stay and stand their ground. If you want to do this, know that you may face some resistance from the bank or new property owner. With that said, until you receive an eviction notice, you cannot be forcefully removed from the property, your utilities cannot be shut off, and the locks cannot be changed on you.

Another option that you have is to approach the financial lender in question. Your best luck is when dealing with either a locally owned or operated bank. When doing so, you will have two different options. Ask to stay in the home or rental unit. Unfortunately, some banks will automatically start the eviction process as soon as a property enters into foreclosure. This is partly due to fear that the property will not promptly sell. Many banks don't want the hassle or liability of having to deal with a renter. If you are a long-term renter, plead your case, which should include prompt and on time rent payments.

Next, you can offer to buy the property. Even if you aren't in the best financial standing or if you are unprepared to make the often required down payment, the lender may be willing to work with you. Once again, your chances improve when dealing with a locally owned or operated bank. If you are a long-term renter and can prove that you have made consistent on time rent payments, have the money needed to pay for a mortgage or home loan, the lender in question may be able to work with you. After all, they want to sell the property and recoup their lost money as quickly as possible.

Although some banks will start the eviction process right away, others will not. This is normally when they believe they can sell the home quickly, like in an auction. If this occurs, you may want to wait and work out an agreement with the new owner. If you are in an apartment complex or a multi-family home, your chances of being able to stay are pretty good. However, if you rent a single family home, the new buyer may intend to move him or herself in.

As an important reminder, you can always throw in the towel and start preparing to move when your rental unit is facing foreclosure, but you don't have to. As a renter, you have a number of legal rights, as well as options.

Chapter 27: Conclusion

There are a number of different events and situations that lead homeowners to the brink of foreclosure, including an unexpected job loss, or even a severe medical emergency. However, a number of other actions, even simply choosing the wrong type of loan when you purchase your home can also send you into similar dire financial territory.

If you should happen to take on a riskier loan, even if you do not have to pay a lot of money right from the start, you can find yourself facing foreclosure, especially if the interest rate on your loan is a variable rate meaning that it can go up when interest rates increase every year.

It does not really matter what the reasons are for your dire financial problems. What does matter is that all is not lost. There are options and alternatives available to you that are well worth trying. You still may be able to save your home, by filing for bankruptcy, or re negotiating your mortgage. If you want to try to save your home by avoiding foreclosure, then you will benefit from some of the strategies in this book.

Keep in mind that avoiding foreclosure is no picnic. You will have to work hard, and be patient, but it is quite possible for many people to do so above all else: Do not give up.

Let's recap what was discussed in the earlier chapters.

We defined mortgage as a type of loan, and the loan is used to purchase a piece of property. The property that is being purchased is treated like a guarantee for the amount of the loan. This guarantee acts as a lien against the property. Once you have signed all of the papers associated with the closing of the sale, the lien will be recorded in public records in the county court house. Until you pay the debt off and have the lien released, you cannot simply sell your home to someone else.

Even when a mortgage is in place and certain actions cannot be taken until the mortgage has been paid in full, you still have full ownership and full title to the property.

The lien being held against the mortgage does, however, give the lender the full right to sell off the secured property to recover his or her funds if you fail to make regular payments on the debt that you owe.

When applying for a mortgage, there are actually a number of different options available to you, including fixed rate mortgages, adjustable rate mortgages, balloon mortgages and interest only mortgages, just to name a few. For more information about these different types of mortgages, see the glossary at the end of this book.

Foreclosure is the process by which your lender can legally take ownership of your home from you, if you should happen to fail to hold up your end of the bargain detailed in your mortgage or deed of trust agreement. Once the lender forecloses upon your home, you have to move out otherwise you will be forcefully evicted.

In addition to losing ownership of your home, you can also lose a lot more. For example, you may still end up owing the lender more money, depending on the value of your home at the time of foreclosure. You will more than likely also destroy your credit rating in the process, which will make it much more difficult to buy a new home in the future.

There are two different types of foreclosure that you can find yourself facing: Judicial foreclosures, and non-judicial foreclosures. In either case, your property will more than likely be seized by the lender and put up for auction, and the highest bidder will become the new owner. In some cases the lender bids on the house during the auction, at whatever price the debt is owed at. If no other buyer bids higher than the lender, the lender wins the property and is able to turn a profit on your home and to get back all of the money that they lost in the transaction.

Pre foreclosure is the time period that exists between the day that the lender notifies you that a foreclosure lawsuit has been filed or the day that a Notice of Default has been filed, and the actual date that the property is slated to be sold at a public auction or in a trustee's sale. Just because you receive a notice like this, it simply does not mean that you have lost the fight.

You still have the possibility of preventing a foreclosure from occurring.

For example, if you want to you can sell the property, or you may consider filing for bankruptcy. You may also consider refinancing, or devising a workout plan with your lender. The most important thing to understand is that all is not lost, and that you still can save your house.

The foreclosure rates are growing rapidly, and the number of homes being foreclosed upon in recent years has shot up significantly from the numbers a decade or two ago. You are not alone in this, and there are hundreds of thousands of other people all over the country who are fighting this same process at the exact same time.

Five states account for more than 50 percent of USA's third quarter 2010 total. California alone accounted for 21 percent of the nation's total foreclosure activity in the third quarter, with 191,016 properties receiving a foreclosure notice, the nation's largest foreclosure activity total. California foreclosure activity decreased nearly 1 percent from the previous quarter and was down nearly 24 percent from the third quarter of 2009.

Florida foreclosure activity increased 12 percent from the previous quarter and was flat from a year ago, giving the state the second largest foreclosure activity total, with 157,026 properties receiving a foreclosure filing.

With 49,103 properties receiving a foreclosure filing in the third quarter, Arizona posted the nation's third largest state foreclosure activity total. Arizona foreclosure activity increased nearly 8 percent from the previous quarter but was down 2 percent from the third quarter of 2009.

Illinois posted the nation's fourth largest foreclosure activity total, with 47,802 properties receiving foreclosure filings, and Michigan posted the nation's fifth largest foreclosure activity total, with 46,100 properties receiving foreclosure filings. Foreclosure activity in both Illinois and Michigan increased on a quarterly and annual basis in the third quarter.

Other states with foreclosure activity totals among the nation's 10 highest were Georgia (41,231), Nevada (38,429), Ohio (36,677), Texas (34,187) and Washington (17,670)

Do not become a statistic, by falling into this drastically growing number of foreclosures. Homeowners and families are not meant to be statistics. Now is your time to act, regardless of whether you are just falling into a debt problem, or have already received a foreclosure lawsuit notice, or a Notice of Default letter.

There is still time to save your home, your credit rating, and your financial situation, as long as you are willing to take the advice presented within these book and to promise not to give up as long as you still have options and alternatives to explore.

Many people have managed to ward off foreclosure by re-negotiating terms with a lender, by declaring bankruptcy, or by selling their homes on their own. There are options available to you, and all is not lost by any means.

Are you ready to figure out what your options are? You need to understand is that not all opportunities out there are legitimate, and yes, there are unfortunately a lot of people out there who want to take advantage of you in your dire financial situation, so watch out for foreclosure scams.

Survive foreclosure and get back on your feet after a foreclosure occurs. Good Luck!

Foreclosure Glossary

Adjustable Rate Mortgage - These are also known as ARMs, and are mortgages that have interest rates that change on a periodic basis. The interest rate is generally pegged to some standard rate when you take this type of loan.

Appraisal - This is a written justification that explains the price that is paid for a specific property. The appraisal is typically based on the analysis of other similar homes that are in the nearby area, or on comparable sales within the community.

Asset - Assets are items that have value and that are owned by a single individual. There are a variety of different types of assets that can be converted directly into cash. These assets are referred to as liquid assets because they can be easily liquefied into cash. Liquid assets include banking accounts, bonds, stocks, mutual funds and many others. Other types of assets include personal property, real estate and debts that are owned to an individual by other individuals.

Assumes and Agrees to Pay - this is a clause that can be found in a number of different types of deeds and related documents, and it states that when the buyer decides to take over the payments that originally belonged to a seller's old mortgage loan, he or she is also agreeing to pay off the old loan in its entirety. The buyer is normally responsible for obtaining the title and then making whatever payments should happen to follow. You can usually find this clause in the section of the document pertaining to the transfer of the title of the property to the buyer from the seller. This clause may or may not completely release the seller from any and all liabilities.

Balloon Mortgage - A balloon mortgage is a mortgage where you pay an agreed upon interest rate on the loan, but only for a pre specified amount of time. At the end of this pre-determined time period, the total amount of the mortgage becomes due. This is a viable lending option for some people, but those facing foreclosure are probably better off not exploring this particular option.

Bankruptcy - After filing in a federal court for bankruptcy proceedings, individuals can either relieve or restructure their liabilities and their debts through the bankruptcy process. There are actually a number of different types of bankruptcies, but the most prevalent are Chapter 7 Bankruptcy which is no asset bankruptcy, and Chapter 13 bankruptcy.

Chapter 7 bankruptcy is capable of relieving most types of debt that the borrower is facing. Borrowers cannot generally become qualified for paper loans for at least two years after the bankruptcy is discharged, and people are required to re-establish their ability to repay debt, meaning that they need to build their credit up again before they will qualify for a mortgage loan.

Chapter 7 - This is a chapter in the Federal Bankruptcy Code that calls for liquidation. What this means, is that any assets that belong to the debtor that are non-exempt will be given up, or sold off for the benefit of whatever creditors are still owed money, in the order of their priority.

In Chapter 7 bankruptcy, the debt is never actually discharged. Secured creditors need to continue to receive their payments or assets to pay off the loans that they are still owed, while unsecured creditors receive very little if anything in return for their loans when Chapter 7 bankruptcy is filed.

Chapter 13 Bankruptcy - This is a chapter of the Federal Bankruptcy Code giving wage earners the ability to reduce debt through court orders according to planned terms that allow debtors to pay much of the original amounts owed if not the total amount owed.

Deed in Lieu - This option may allow you to "give back" the property to your lender voluntarily, without damaging your credit further than you already have. Lenders can decide from this point whether they want to cease the foreclosure activity if the borrower asks to provide this option.

Deed of Trust - In nearly half of all of the United States, deeds of trust are used rather than mortgages. However, just like mortgages, deeds of trust are recorded in public records so that everyone will know that a lien is placed on your property.

Three parties are involved in the deed of trust: You are the trustor, as the homeowner who took the loan out, then there is a beneficiary, which is the financial institution providing the money for the loan, and finally there is a neutral third party known as the trustee.

Equity - This is a home owner's financial interest in a particular piece of property. Equity is calculated as the real difference that exists between the fair market value on a property, and the amount of money that is still owned on its mortgage loan, and on any other liens that are attached to it.

Fixed Rate Mortgage - This is a mortgage where the interest rate is set when you first take the loan, and then it remains the same throughout the entire length of the loan.

Forbearance - This occurs when the lender voluntarily accepts to take lower payments than what was originally agreed to in the documents for the loan, but only for a specific period of time so that the borrower can recover financially from a job loss or some other financial issue.

Foreclosure - Foreclosure is defined as the local process or processes by which a borrower who has defaulted on a mortgage loan is deprived of their ownership rights to the mortgaged property. What this typically involves is the forced sale of the property at a trustee's sale or public auction. The proceeds of the sale are then applied to the debt that has been accrued by the mortgage.

Interest Only Mortgage - These are mortgages where you only pay the interest portion of the loan, and your payment does not include any part of the principal portion of the mortgage loan.

Lender - This is a term that refers to the institutions that make loans, along with any other individuals that represent the firm that makes the loan. Loan officers and lending companies are both commonly referred to as lenders.

Lien - Liens are defined as legal claims that are made against properties. Liens need to be paid off completely in full any time that the property is sold. Mortgages and first trust needs are normally considered to be liens.

Mortgage - A mortgage is a type of loan, and the loan is used to purchase a piece of property. The property that is being purchased is treated like a guarantee for the amount of the loan. This guarantee acts as a lien against the property.

Principal - The principal part of the loan is the amount that is borrowed, or rather the amount that was borrowed but that still remains unpaid. The principal is also regarded as the part of a monthly payment that actually reduces the balance of the mortgage that is actually still remaining to be paid, not including the interest rate or the interest that was accrued.

Real Estate Agent - A real estate agent is a person who has obtained the proper licensing to negotiate and to transact in all of the steps that are normally associated with selling real estate property. Real estate agents can deal in residential property, commercial property or a combination of the two.

Real Property - In essence, the concept of "real property" falls into the scope of any items that have tangible ownership capability. This includes land, and including anything that has a permanent nature like rocks, landscaping, trees, and structures and so on.

Realtor - Realtors are real estate agents, real estate associations, real estate associates and real estate brokers who hold an active membership in one or more of any local real estate boards. The real estate board has to be accredited and affiliated with the National Association of Realtors to qualify.

Second Mortgage - Second mortgages are mortgages that have lean positions that act as subordinate mortgages to the first mortgage. Second mortgages can be used either to reduce or to improve the terms of the first mortgage, or to draw an amount of cash out of the original mortgage based in the form of equity in the home. When it comes to foreclosure proceedings, the lender with the first mortgage always has precedence over the lender dealing with the second mortgage.

Short Sale - This is a specific type of workout procedure that involves the lender accepting less than the full balance due on the loan. This is an option made available to homeowners who want to sell their home quickly and for less than the fair market value of the property in order to avoid the proceedings dealing with foreclosure.

Title - The title is a legal document that exists to clearly evidence a person's right to the express ownership of a piece of property. Titles are most commonly used for vehicles and properties.

Two Step Mortgage - Two step mortgages are adjustable rate mortgages, or ARM mortgages that have a single interest rate for the first five or seven years of length for the mortgage term, and then the interest rate changes for the remainder of the amortization term of the mortgage to reflect a different interest rate all together. The two very different mortgage rates are what make this a "two step" mortgage.

Wage Earner's Plan - The Wage Earner's Plan is just another nickname for the Chapter 13 division of bankruptcy proceedings.

Warranty Deed - A warranty deed is a conveyance of land, and involves the grantor guaranteeing the title of the land to the grantee.

Without Recourse - These are words that are most commonly used in the process of endorsing either a note or a bill. The note or bill is endorsed to denote that the future holder of a piece of property is not allowed to turn to the endorser in the event that there is an issue with making payment on time.

Workout - A workout is a process by which a borrower or home owner comes to a mutually acceptable arrangement on a financial basis with the lender of a deed or mortgage as a means of avoiding a foreclosure on the horizon. Not all lenders offer workout plans, but many are more than willing to help borrowers overcome their financial issues to avoid foreclosure.

Wrap Around - This is a specific type of mortgage that involves the obligation to pay later liens including the obligation to also pay earlier lien mortgages at the same time. Essentially speaking, the later mortgage is wrapped around the earlier mortgage, and any defaults that are placed on the earlier lien or mortgage are automatically defaulted on the later lien mortgages as well.

Wrap Around Loan - A wrap around loan is a newer type of loan, and it encompasses any and all existing loans, passing defaults from older loans onto the new loans in the process.

Wrongful Foreclosure - This is a type of foreclosure that in some way or another was legally improper. Wrongful foreclosure is a foreclosure that caused a borrower to needlessly suffer wrongful and purely unnecessary damages.

Good Luck!